Understanding Violent Behavior

Christine Wilcox

San Diego, CA

About the Author

Christine Wilcox writes fiction and nonfiction for young adults and adults. She has worked as an editor, an instructional designer, and a writing instructor. She lives in Richmond, Virginia, with her husband, David, and her son, Doug.

LIBRARY OF CONGRESS CATALOGING-IN-PUBLICATION DATA

Name: Wilcox, Christine, author.
Title: Understanding Violent Behavior/by Christine Wilcox.
Description: San Diego, CA: ReferencePoint Press, Inc., 2018. | Series:
  Understanding Psychology | Includes bibliographical references and index.
Identifiers: LCCN 2017011641 (print) | LCCN 2017021009 (ebook) | ISBN
  9781682822845 (eBook) | ISBN 9781682822838 (hardback)
Subjects: LCSH: Aggressiveness—Juvenile literature. |
  Violence—Psychological aspects—Juvenile literature.
Classification: LCC BF575.A3 (ebook) | LCC BF575.A3 W55 2018 (print) | DDC
  155.2/32--dc23
LC record available at https://lccn.loc.gov/2017011641

CONTENTS

The Human Brain: Thought, Behavior, and Emotion

Frontal lobe controls:
- Thinking
- Planning
- Organizing
- Problem solving
- Short-term memory
- Movement
- Personality
- Emotions
- Behavior
- Language

Parietal lobe:
- Interprets sensory information such as taste, temperature, and touch

Temporal lobe:
- Processes information from the senses of smell, taste, and hearing
- Plays role in memory storage

Occipital lobe:
- Processes images from the eyes
- Links information with images stored in memory

Source: Mayo Foundation for Education and Research, "Slide Show: How Your Brain Works." www.mayoclinic.org.

INTRODUCTION

Is Violent Behavior Declining?

Scientists agree that violence is one of the defining features of humanity. The *Homo sapiens* species is particularly violent when compared to most other mammals. Only about 0.3 percent of all mammalian deaths are caused by same-species violence, but primates—like gorillas, chimps, and human beings—kill each other at a rate that is nearly six times higher. While humans are not the most murderous species (that dubious honor goes to the meerkat), they are unusually violent. As neuroscientist R. Douglas Fields describes:

> Slaughter is a defining behavior of our species. We kill all other creatures, and we kill our own. . . . Carnivores kill for food; we kill our family members, our children, our parents, our spouses, our brothers and sisters, our cousins and in-laws. We kill strangers. We kill people who are different from us, in appearance, beliefs, race, and social status. . . . Grandparents, parents, fathers, mothers—all kill and all of them are the targets of killing.[1]

Why Are Humans So Violent?

Fields and other researchers believe that three factors combine to make humans especially violent. Humans are extremely social, highly territorial, and unusually intelligent. Because they are both social and territorial, they are psychologically predisposed to join

5

social groups and to defend their territory and resources against outsiders. And because they are intelligent, they have the ability to carefully plan these acts of violence and to invent deadly and efficient ways of killing.

However, the factors leading to group-on-group violence do not explain violence between individuals—which can escalate from minor disagreements to deadly encounters in the blink of an eye. This type of violence is driven by rage—an emotional response to threat that compels people to lash out against one another, sometimes with deadly results. Rage-induced violence is extremely common. As journalist Jennifer Mascia points out about gun violence, "It's the shootings taking place in parking lots, bars, schools, bedrooms, and street corners across America that are responsible for most gun injuries and deaths."[2] Though her example focuses on a specific kind of violence, her point can be applied to humans' violent behavior in general. It is the people who ordinarily

Police officers in Chicago investigate a shooting death. Rage between individuals, which can escalate in seconds, is responsible for most gun injuries and deaths in the United States.

do not engage in criminally violent behavior—people with families, jobs, and ties to the community—who are responsible for most of the violence among humans.

Empathy: The Antidote to Violence

Even though humans have a propensity for violence, they also have a natural aversion to killing. Few people will voluntarily harm or kill another human being if they, or their group, are not under threat. Killing is repellent to most people—in part because of the human ability to empathize. Empathy allows a person not only to imagine what another is feeling, but to actually experience those feelings. This ability is encoded in the human brain and allows humans to bond with each other, care for each other, and form lasting relationships.

Empathy also encourages people to cooperate in social groups, which gives humans a nonviolent way to increase and protect their resources. Many scientists believe that humans benefit more from cooperating and sharing than they do from using violence to acquire and defend resources. As biologist Luke Glowacki explains, "Just as groups may fight because of environmental pressures or resource scarcity, they may also have strong incentives to expand trade relations and build alliances that benefit both parties. The capacity for peaceful and cooperative relationships was surely more essential for the survival and success of the species than bellicosity."[3] If people usually benefit more from cooperation than they do from conflict, it makes sense that the human brain has evolved to avoid violence when possible.

Violence in Society Is Decreasing

Today humans are cooperating with each other at unprecedented levels. Despite that fact, people tend to believe that the world is becoming an increasingly violent and dangerous place. Every day, the media reports dozens of senseless acts of violence and brutality. As psychologist Steven Pinker notes, "Anyone who has followed the news knows that this doesn't appear to be a particularly peaceful time."[4]

However, Pinker, who has studied worldwide trends in violence extensively, claims that the idea that violence is increasing is actually an illusion. The media tends to report violence that is both unusual and shocking, such as terrorist attacks, mass shootings, and police shootings of civilians. Even though these acts of violence are prominently covered in the news, they represent only a tiny fraction of violent incidents overall, and these more common incidents have been in steady decline for years. "Reporters give lavish coverage to gun bursts, explosions, and viral videos, oblivious to how representative they are," says Pinker. "The world is not falling apart. The kinds of violence to which most people are vulnerable—homicide, rape, battering, child abuse—have been in steady decline. . . . Wars between states [nations]—by far the most destructive of all conflicts—are all but obsolete."[5]

For example, gun homicides in the United States have been declining for decades. According to the FBI, from 1993 to 2014 (the most recent year for which data is available), gun homicides dropped by more than half, and the overall homicide rate in the United States was at a fifty-one-year low. Global violence due to war is also declining. According to the Peace Research Institute Oslo, in 1950 there were between 557,000 and 851,000 battle deaths. The Uppsala Conflict Data Program estimates that by 2013 (the most recent year for which worldwide data is available), battle deaths had decreased to about 30,000. As Pinker explains, "Today we are probably living in the most peaceful time in our species' existence."[6]

Why Are Humans Less Violent Today?

Scientists do not know precisely why violence has been decreasing so dramatically in recent years, but some scientists have come up with a theory to explain the trend. They suggest that the decrease in violence corresponds with the rise in connectedness among peoples across the world. Connection through globalization, or international trade, has reduced conflicts between nations. As Pinker explains, "The incentives for conquest and invasion have been outnumbered by the incentives to make business—what that means is that a person alive is worth more to me than a dead one, or buying a good is easier than stealing one."[7] Also, technologies like the Internet allow people from different nations to form relationships. Books and movies are also now distributed internationally, which exposes people to other cultures and allows them to understand the interior lives of different types of people. According to psychologist Steve Taylor, this increased interconnection "promotes moral inclusion, an expansion of empathy, and makes it less possible for us to perceive different groups as 'other' to us. It helps us to sense that, even if they appear culturally or racially different, all human beings are essentially the same as us."[8]

Though humanity's increased interconnectedness fosters empathy and reduces violence, humans are still extremely social, highly territorial, and unusually intelligent. Those combined factors continue to create violence between people. And humans still have brains that were designed to respond to threats with violence. People kill outsiders they see as a threat, either in cities or on the battlefield, and they kill people close to them when enraged. Increased interconnectedness is helping to decrease these incidences, yet violence remains a serious problem for humanity.

CHAPTER 1

The Brain, Evolution, and the Rage Response

Most people are shocked when an ordinary, nonviolent person commits a horrendous act of violence. Their first instinct is to look for an explanation—perhaps the person just suffered a loss, is mentally ill, or is in the grips of religious mania. However, the likely explanation is that the individual was simply overcome by rage. Rage is an automatic response to threat that humans have evolved to protect themselves and their loved ones from danger. When people are enraged, they are capable of superhuman acts of strength, speed, and stamina. All humans have the capacity for rage. And when rage gets out of control, it can be deadly.

The Human Brain

Before discussing the rage response, it is important to understand how the brain works. The human brain is an extremely complex organ—the most complicated structure in the known universe. It is made up of about 100 billion neurons, or nerve cells, that control everything that happens in the human body. Each neuron is highly specialized and works in conjunction with other neurons, sending chemical messages throughout the body via the nervous system. To send these messages, each neuron connects with as many as 10,000 other neurons, creating an unimaginably complex network made up of about 100 trillion connections.

Neurons connect to each other by growing threadlike structures (called axons) that reach out to receptor threads (called dendrites) of targeted neurons. Some of these threads are microscopic, while others can be several feet long. Axons and dendrites do not actually touch each other; instead, they leave a microscopic space between them called a synapse. Once a group of neurons are connected, they communicate with each other by releasing a type of chemical known as a neurotransmitter into the synapse. The neurotransmitter is like a control switch; for instance, some neurotransmitters increase attention, some are involved in creating emotions like love or sadness or anger, and some activate various chemical processes in the body.

All of this activity is powered by electrical charges created inside the neurons. This allows information to be communicated throughout the brain and body extremely rapidly. In addition, neurons are constantly connecting and disconnecting with each

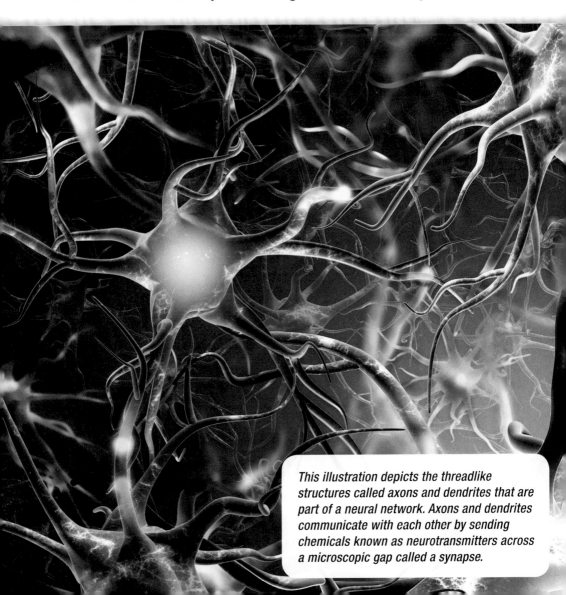

This illustration depicts the threadlike structures called axons and dendrites that are part of a neural network. Axons and dendrites communicate with each other by sending chemicals known as neurotransmitters across a microscopic gap called a synapse.

other based on sensory input and experiences. The pathways also grow stronger or weaker, depending on how often they are used. This process, called neuroplasticity or brain plasticity, allows humans to mature, learn, and change. This complex web of ever-changing neural pathways gives rise to thought, memory, emotion, and consciousness.

Some neural pathways are hardwired in the human brain, meaning that the pathways are genetically determined and are part of the brain's basic design. Threat detection pathways evolved in our ancestors hundreds of thousands of years ago to detect dangerous situations and ensure survival. Like the neural pathways that automatically keep the heart pumping and the lungs expanding and contracting, the pathways of threat detection and response can operate independently of human thought. Once triggered, they can activate what scientists refer to as the rage response—the powerful and instinctual emotional reaction that drives spontaneous acts of violence. Rage arises automatically, but in many cases—especially when the danger is not immediate or life threatening—the urge to respond with violence can be controlled or suppressed by the thinking part of the brain. And because of brain plasticity, people can weaken and change the neural pathways that control the rage response so that the pathways are not activated inappropriately.

Violence and the Amygdala

The brain structure involved in threat detection and the rage response is called the amygdala. The amygdala is made up of two small, almond-shaped structures located deep within the brain. These structures are part of the limbic system—the portion of the brain involved in generating emotion. While the function of the amygdala is complex, scientists believe it is primarily involved in generating strong, primary emotions, such as fear and rage. Aggression and violence, scientists believe, begin in the amygdala. When assessing and responding to threats, the amygdala communicates with the rest of the brain in an extremely complex and sophisticated way. Working in conjunction with other parts of the brain, it evaluates information from all five senses, accesses memories and stored knowledge, and if necessary, takes control of the motor system.

Neuroscientist R. Douglas Fields has intimate experience with the complexity of the brain's threat detection and rage response system. While on vacation in Barcelona, Spain, he and his daughter were walking on a crowded street. Suddenly, Fields felt a tug on his pant leg and realized his wallet had just been stolen. In an instant he shot his hand backward, hooked his

Meditation Calms Rage

One excellent therapy to tame rage is meditation. Meditation allows its practitioners to have greater conscious control over their thought processes. During practice, when their thoughts drift away from the object of their focus (for instance, their breathing), practitioners re-center their attention. The mental exercise of observing thoughts and refocusing attention has remarkable effects on the brain. Studies have shown that meditation actually increases the number of neurons and neural pathways involved with calmness and focus and decreases those involved with anger, fear, and anxiety. For instance, a 2011 study at Harvard University found that after completing an eight-week meditation class, participants had fewer neurons and neural activity in their amygdalas. "It is fascinating to see the brain's plasticity and that, by practicing meditation, we can play an active role in changing the brain and can increase our well-being and quality of life," says psychologist Britta Hölzel, one of the authors of the study.

Quoted in Brent Lambert, "Harvard Unveils MRI Study Proving Meditation Literally Rebuilds the Brain's Gray Matter in 8 Weeks," *FEELguide*, November 19, 2014. www.feelguide.com.

arm around the pickpocket's neck, and threw him to the ground, where he pinned him to the pavement in a headlock. He was able to respond so quickly because his unconscious brain—specifically, his amygdala—had detected the pickpocket and had primed his body for a violent response.

At the time, Fields was fifty-six years old and weighed 130 pounds (59 kg), and his last physical confrontation had been on the high school wrestling team. The man he attacked was young and strong, yet Fields was able to immediately overpower him and recover his wallet with no conscious thought or planning. "The rage reflex can unleash furious, uncontrollable anger," Fields explains, "[or it can] trigger a rage of intense and purposeful violence devoid of anger. In either case the response is automatic and apparently unchecked by rational thought."[9]

Fight or Flight Versus Free Will

The rage response is part of the fight-or-flight response—the urge to either fight or flee in a dangerous situation. When the amygdala detects a threat, it directs chemicals like adrenaline and cortisol to flood the body, pulling blood into muscles, speeding up breathing and heart rate, and priming the body to either attack or escape. In this state humans can suddenly have tremendous strength and speed as the body delegates all of its resources toward surviving the threat at hand.

In humans the hardwired fight-or-flight response can be consciously suppressed—especially if the threat does not require immediate lifesaving action. This conscious control derives from a highly specialized part of the brain called the cerebral cortex. The cerebral cortex is the outer layer of the brain and is responsible for conscious thought and free will. The ability to suppress urges like the fight-or-flight response is controlled by a part of the cerebral cortex located right behind the forehead, called the prefrontal

A threatening situation, such as being bullied, prompts a physical reaction known as the fight-or-flight response. This response causes physiological changes that prepare the body to either fight or flee the perceived threat.

cortex. This area is involved in planning, goal-directed behavior, and resisting urges or impulses.

After Fields retrieved his wallet from the pickpocket, to continue the example, he was finally able to access his prefrontal cortex. He could see that he was not out of danger; the pickpocket had been working with a gang of other young men, who now surrounded Fields and his daughter. By this time Fields's body

Heroes and the Rage Response

On Christmas Day 2009, Nigerian-born Umar Farouk Abdulmutallab attempted to blow up Northwest Airlines Flight 253 over Detroit, Michigan. Abdulmutallab had sewn part of a bomb into his undergarments, and it had not been noticed by security. When he attempted to explode the bomb with a handheld detonation device, the device began to smoke and caught fire.

One of the passengers, Dutch filmmaker Jasper Schuringa, saw that Abdulmutallab was holding a suspicious-looking device in his hand and was surrounded by smoke and fire. Schuringa jumped over the seat in front of him, yanked the object from Abdulmutallab's hand, and put out the fire. When Schuringa was asked later why he ran toward danger and the other passengers did not, he replied, "I don't know, I didn't think."

Schuringa's automatic act of heroism was generated by the same part of the brain that controls the rage response. "We have these circuits to protect ourselves, our family unit, or society," explains neuroscientist R. Douglas Fields. "Most of the time, they work amazingly well. We don't call it snapping [in rage] unless the result of this aggressive response is inappropriate. When it works as intended we call it quick thinking or, in many cases, heroic."

Quoted in Simon Worrall, "Your Brain Is Hardwired to Snap," National Geographic, February 7, 2016. http://news.nationalgeographic.com.

was flooded with adrenaline and cortisol, and he was primed to attack. He recalls his thought processes at the time:

> A massive surge of adrenaline fueled my twitching muscles and nerves to levels of raw power I had never felt before. I was now struggling not to pick up the next hoodlum squaring off with me, hoist him over my head, and hurl him into his accomplices. . . . It was not a question of whether I could execute the superhuman feat. I had no doubt that I could do it. Rather, I was trying not to do it, simply because this might not be my best option.[10]

Fields used his prefrontal cortex to suppress the violent urges generated by his amygdala until he could decide on the safest thing to do. Luckily, the criminals were distracted by a passerby, allowing him and his daughter to escape.

Fields says that he wishes he had had access to his prefrontal cortex earlier, because then he could have resisted the urge toward violence altogether. It would have been much safer, he says, if he had simply allowed the pickpocket to take his wallet and not fought back. Instead, he fell under the power of an ancient, instinctual reflex—to protect his resources at any cost.

Rage in the Modern World

In early humans the rage response was crucial for survival. When a person was under attack by a wild animal or another human, there was no time to consciously assess the situation and decide what to do. Therefore, the brain developed a defensive system that automatically springs into action in response to danger. Evolutionary biologists believe that this danger did not need to be physical to trigger the reaction. Intrusions on territory, perceived threats to family members or one's community, or even insults were—and still are—perceived as deadly threats by the brain.

Even though modern humans face far fewer dangers than their ancestors, the human rage response still interprets some threats as potentially life threatening. Most people have experienced the rage response in their day-to-day lives and know how powerful it can be. Small disagreements suddenly escalate into shouting matches; parents lash out at their children after a stressful day; people ruin each other's reputations online in a fit of anger or jealousy. And even among law-abiding individuals, the rage response can occasionally turn violent. Shouting matches can turn into physical fights. Enraged parents can hurt their children. And if a weapon is at hand, anger or jealousy can quickly turn deadly.

In his book *Why We Snap: Understanding the Rage Circuit in Your Brain*, Fields presents the idea that there are universal triggers for rage and violence among human beings. He groups the triggers into nine general categories that can be remembered with the acronym LIFEMORTS. They are Life-or-limb (a physical attack),

Insult (a challenge to dominance), Family (a threat to blood relatives), Environment (a threat to one's territory), Mate (rage triggered by jealousy), Order in society (an urge to punish those who disrupt society), Resources (a threat to one's belongings), Tribe (a threat from another group), and Stopped (rage triggered by being restrained, either physically or by oppression).

The triggers of rage often layer one on top of another, causing frustration to build until a person snaps, or explodes in a fit of violence. While this may have been a useful response for early humans fighting for survival, in modern times rage and aggression are often counterproductive. Fields notes that most of the time, when modern humans experience bouts of rage, they do or say things they deeply regret.

Road Rage

One example of how these triggers can be activated in modern society—sometimes with deadly results—is the phenomenon of road rage. Fields explains that the act of driving a car can activate nearly every one of the LIFEMORTS rage triggers. Imagine, for instance, that a woman driving with her children is cut off in traffic. The other driver has put her and her family in danger (Life-or-limb and Family); has nearly hit her car (Resources); has cut in line, infringing on her territory (Environment); has broken the law (Order in society); and has slowed her progress (Stopped). Now imagine that the other driver is a different race or class than the woman (Tribe) and makes an obscene gesture as she cuts the woman off (Insult). In this very common scenario, all but the Mate (jealousy) trigger has been activated. If the woman is already frustrated by traffic—and therefore has a lowered threshold for stress—she may be overcome with rage.

According to Fields, acts of spontaneous rage and aggression like road rage happen constantly in modern society. When they cause a deadly tragedy, people tend to assume that some sort of mental illness or other underlying pathology is involved, but this is rarely the case. "The commonplace blind rage attacks between spouses, coworkers, and complete strangers are the cause of far more aggression and violence than that caused by the mentally ill or psychopathic killer,"[11] Fields explains.

The modern phenomenon known as road rage results from what some researchers believe are universal triggers for rage and violence. According to this theory, the act of driving a car can activate nearly every one of these triggers.

Violence Caused by Unregulated Rage

Even though most people have experienced the rage response, few behave so violently that they run afoul of the police or harm another person. Most people are able to use their prefrontal cortex to control their aggression. Those who do inflict violence on others—people whom we think of as violent criminals— sometimes have characteristics that might explain their violent actions, such as a history of childhood abuse or mental illness. However, most people who have been abused as children or suffer from mental illness do not commit violent acts, and psychologists agree that in the vast majority of cases, abuse or mental illness do not in themselves cause people to be violent. "Violent crimes committed by people with mental illness get a lot of attention," says psychologist Laura Hayes. "But they are rare enough that if all the violent crime perpetrated by those with mental illness were eliminated, 96 percent of violent crime would continue."[12]

The one thing that almost all violent criminals have in common is an inability to control their rage response. "Violent crimes are committed by people who lack the ability to regulate and modulate their response to perceived danger,"[13] explains Hayes. Because of this, nearly all violent criminals have a history of escalating violent behavior. For instance, 80 percent to 90 percent of murderers have police records, as compared to 15 percent of the general population. And when one spouse kills another, there is a nine in ten chance that there was previous violence in the household.

As Hayes explains, "The individual who lacks the essential skill of using more sophisticated reasoning, perspective-taking, and emotional stabilization to regulate his more primitive fear and aggressive impulses will fall into the pattern of aggressive overreaction again and again, often with escalating levels of violence."[14] In other words, people who cannot use their prefrontal cortex to control their rage response are the ones who become criminally violent. They may also have a history of early exposure to violence or a mental illness, but their lack of anger management skills is what precipitates violence.

Getting Control of Rage

One way to reduce violence in society is to identify people who cannot control their anger and give them skills to calm their rage response. Many psychologists believe that children and adolescents should be taught anger management techniques such as breathing deeply, redirecting their thoughts, and practicing compassion for others before violence becomes a habitual response. According to psychologist Melanie Greenberg, these techniques work for adults as well and can help "retrain our minds so we are less likely to overreact with intense anger or fear to psychological threats."[15] Because of brain plasticity, people have the ability to learn new responses to stress and frustration, and with practice, these new responses can replace the rage response.

> **WORDS IN CONTEXT**
>
> **brain plasticity**
> The brain's ability to make or break connections between neurons, which allows humans to learn, change, and grow. Also known as neuroplasticity.

CHAPTER 2

Violence and the Outsider

Early humans lived in groups that scientists call "tribes"—bands of hunter-gatherers who shared common ancestry, culture, and beliefs. During this period of history, the environment was harsh and dangerous, and people needed to live in groups to survive. Tribes could hunt more efficiently, share resources, and protect each other from predatory animals and other humans. For these reasons, humans have evolved a deep psychological need to find acceptance within a larger group and to defend that group from others. According to biologist Luke Glowacki, scientists believe that "the human propensity for lethal violence against 'out-group' members has deep evolutionary roots."[16] In other words, tribalism and the violence it can lead to are psychologically hardwired into the human brain.

In modern times this predisposition toward tribalism explains why people can be suspicious and hostile toward those of different races, classes, religions, or nationalities. Tribalism drives racism, hate crimes, and warfare. In fact, the desire to protect and defend one's group can become a moral justification for violence—even among people who believe that violence is morally wrong.

In-Groups and Out-Groups

Social scientists use the terms *in-group* and *out-group* when describing the human tendency to identify with a particular tribe or group of people. Humans identify with others based on things like appearance and kinship (or family ties), culture, nationality, ideology, and political or religious beliefs. For most of human history, people

organized themselves into tribes based on appearance and kinship, most likely because people who are related to each other tend to take care of each other, providing group security. As human populations grew and more diverse people joined together, religious beliefs came to define a group's identity. According to Jared Diamond, author of *Guns, Germs, and Steel*, "Religion helps solve the problem of how unrelated individuals are to live together without killing each other."[17] As societies and nation-states formed, things like cultural practices and ideologies became part of a group's social identity.

Because competition over territory and resources was a reality for the earliest human tribes, group membership provided not only safety from other groups but solidarity—an "us-versus-them" mind-set that helped group members work together to protect themselves. Therefore, distrust of people in out-groups evolved alongside an affinity for in-groups.

This has resulted in a psychological drive in humans to belong to an in-group and in an innate distrust of members of out-groups. Scientists have concluded that these drives are not products of rational decision making or conscious choice. When scientists randomly assign people into groups, in-group and out-group behaviors naturally arise. Even when the differences between groups are entirely random and meaningless, people still tend to try to help their own group and harm the out-group. For instance, a famous study in 1954 called the Robbers Cave experiment found that preteen boys in a camp setting bonded with their group members and began to distrust another group in a faraway portion of the camp. When games were set up between the competing groups, the competition quickly devolved into aggressive behavior: The boys fought, stole from each other, and organized raids on the other camp.

Similar behaviors have been replicated in dozens of studies. Scientists have even observed this behavior in babies as young as nine months old. A series of psychological experiments at Yale University in 2012 demonstrated that babies prefer puppets that have been linked with foods that they like (graham crackers) and actively dislike puppets linked with foods they dislike (green beans). According to psychologist Paul Bloom, the study found that babies "actually prefer puppets who punish the puppet with the different food taste."[18] This study and many others like it support the idea that aggression toward out-group members is hardwired into the human brain.

> **WORDS IN CONTEXT**
>
> **tribalism**
> Strong loyalty to one's group, involving behaviors and attitudes that support the group and protect it against competing groups.

Prejudice and Violence

Unconscious prejudice based on general appearance is another sign of humanity's distrust of the out-group. Studies have shown that humans make all sorts of assumptions about others based on their appearance—usually in a matter of seconds. "You like faces that are closer to your own definition of a typical face," explains psychologist Alexander Todorov. "It's like a tribal bias. I like people that look like the people around me."[19] This split-second decision making gives rise to all sorts of biases and prejudices that often operate on an unconscious level. For instance, racial prejudice, which is strongly associated with differences in appearance, can be at work within people who have no awareness of any prejudicial feelings within themselves. Studies have shown that managers who are reviewing the résumés of job candidates will be biased for and against candidates based on their assumptions about the race of the applicant—even when the résumés are identical in every other way. In many cases these managers are honestly unaware that they hold any racial prejudices at all.

WORDS IN CONTEXT

bias

A preference for or an aversion to a group, idea, or practice. While bias is not necessarily negative, the term is often used to mean that something is being unfairly judged.

In modern society, group membership is defined by a host of factors, but the most common is differences in racial appearance. Scientists now know that racial appearance has nothing to do with differences in the underlying biology of humans and that race is not defined by genetics. As sociologist Justin Berg explains, "We see millions of people who have the same skin color separate themselves into many different racial groups, or into more than one racial group. This is the opposite outcome of what we'd expect if biology determined our racial identities."[20] However, people still tend to use racial characteristics to decide if a person should be accepted into a group or excluded. Assigning out-group status to those of different races has led to horrendous acts of oppression and brutality. Some examples from US history, in which Caucasian people have historically held power, include the extermination of Native Americans and the enslavement of African Americans.

Split-second decisions based on racial appearance can also cause fear-based violence. A 2015 study published in the *Journal of Experimental Social Psychology* examined forty-two studies

Demonstrators in New York City's Times Square protest the deaths of people killed by law enforcement personnel. Many of the victims were African American; research suggests that unconscious racial bias may have played a role in these incidents.

of racial shooter bias, or the tendency to feel more threatened by people who belong to a particular racial group. The study found that people playing a first-person shooter video game were more likely to shoot computer-generated assailants who had dark skin. According to Yara Mekawi, the study's author, "People were quicker to shoot black targets with a gun, relative to white targets with a gun. And . . . people were more trigger-happy when shooting black targets compared to shooting white targets."[21] Mekawi believes that this unconscious racial bias may be behind the rash of police shootings of unarmed African Americans in the United States.

Ordered to Kill

Out-group violence can also be motivated by a desire to help one's in-group work toward a common ideological goal. For

Male Aggression Benefits the Tribe

In primates and many other social mammals, the male of the species is larger, stronger, and more aggressive than the female. In humans males are about 8 percent taller and 20 percent heavier than females. They also have more of the hormone testosterone, which increases aggression. This difference between the sexes is known as sexual dimorphism, and it is thought to be a reproductive strategy. Males who must compete for females in a group need to be able to fight other males, and the strongest and most aggressive male passes on his genes.

However, males also use their extra size and increased aggressiveness to benefit the tribe. According to Dorian Furtuna, an ethologist who studies the evolutionary roots of human aggression, "In many animal species, including primates, males have the biological role of being guardians of the territory and of banishing the intruders or of protecting the group from predators, and these functions imply that males exhibit a higher level of aggression than females." This social component to male aggression would have made evolutionary sense for early humans. The women, who were weaker and less aggressive, would care for the children and take care of the tribe's other needs, while the men were free to use their strength and aggressiveness to hunt and defend the tribe from invaders.

Dorian Furtuna, "Male Aggression," *Homo Aggressivus* (blog), *Psychology Today*, September 22, 2014. www.psychologytoday.com.

instance, many people fight wars because they believe that violence is necessary to ensure the survival of their country—even though they do not feel immediately threatened by an enemy. They will follow their leader's orders to accomplish this goal, even though it might be emotionally difficult for them to harm other human beings.

This idea was tested in 1961 by psychologist Stanley Milgram. Milgram wanted to understand the actions of the thousands of German soldiers involved in atrocities in the Nazi death camps in the 1940s. He suspected that these ordinary soldiers—loving family men, in many cases—systematically murdered millions of men, women, and children not because they were evil (as most people believed), but because they were ordered to do so by a higher authority—Adolf Hitler and the leaders of the Third Reich. A powerful group leader, Milgram thought, could persuade group members to abandon their morality and follow any order, no matter how morally repugnant.

In his experiment Milgram told participants that they were assisting in an important experiment that tested learning and memory (this was not true). Under the supervision of a scientist, a participant (dubbed the "teacher") tested the memory of a "learner" who was hooked up to an electric shock machine in the next room. The teacher was instructed to ask the learner (via intercom) to memorize and repeat a string of words. When the learner got an answer wrong, the teacher was instructed to deliver an increasingly painful shock to the learner.

The teacher did not know that the learner was actually an actor who was only pretending to be shocked. As the "shocks" grew more painful and dangerous, the learner screamed in pain and begged for the experiment to end. When participants expressed their concern, the scientist simply emphasized how important it was for the experiment to go on. Some participants refused to continue, but many continued to shock the learner, even after he cried out that he had a heart condition—and then fell ominously silent.

The results of the experiment were unsettling. Most of the participants were upset about what they were asked to do. Still, an alarming percentage continued to deliver what they thought were increasingly dangerous shocks. In fact, in one version of the experiment, 65 percent of participants delivered the maximum shock of 450 volts to the learner. As editor Cari Romm writes in the *Atlantic*, the participants "had just been used to prove the claim that would soon make Milgram famous: that ordinary people, under the direction of an authority figure, would obey just about any order they were given, even to torture. . . . If the Nazis were just following orders, then he [Milgram] had just proved that anyone at all could be a Nazi."[22] In other words, Milgram had shown that most people were capable of extreme violence if they were under orders from a higher authority.

Rethinking Milgram

In recent years psychologists have begun to question Milgram's conclusions. Psychologist Alex Haslam does not think that Milgram's participants were simply following orders. Instead, Haslam believed that they were identifying with the scientist and his goals.

Haslam examined Milgram's data and found this to be the case; he discovered that the likelihood that a participant would follow directions and deliver a shock depended on how much he or she believed in the importance of the experiment—and by extension, the goals of science itself, which the scientist represented. This is called social identification, a term meaning that a person's beliefs are drawn from the group with which they identify. Therefore, participants who identified with the scientist continued to deliver shocks—even though harming another person was morally uncomfortable for them. They also did not regret their actions after the experiment was over. According to Haslam, "They did not think they had done anything wrong. This was largely due to Milgram's ability to convince them that they had made an important contribution to science."[23]

Haslam explains that people who commit violence because their group leader orders them to do so "are generally motivated, not by a desire to do evil, but by a sense that what they are doing is worthy and noble."[24] He and his colleagues concluded that a person's "willingness to perform unpleasant tasks [i.e., violence against others] is contingent upon identification with collective goals" of the group, thereby making violence "seem virtuous rather than vicious."[25] In other words, violence can seem morally acceptable if it is done for the good of the group.

One horrific example of this can be seen in the way Germany justified killing children during the Holocaust. On May 5, 1944, Heinrich Himmler, a high-ranking leader of the Nazi Party, gave a speech in which he defended the murder of Jewish children in the German death camps: "In my view, we as Germans, however deeply we may feel in our hearts, are not entitled to allow a generation of avengers filled with hatred to grow up with whom our children and grandchildren will have to deal because we, too weak and cowardly, left it to them."[26] In other words, Himmler was saying that soldiers who endure the emotional pain of murdering innocent children are making a noble sacrifice for future generations of Germans.

Dehumanization

Despite the natural tendency to distrust and fear people who are not part of their groups, most people do not find it easy to deliberately harm or kill others without provocation. Humans have a great capacity for empathy. For instance, most people feel bad

The Power of Masks

When people gather together, they become more likely to take on the values and behaviors of the group around them. This psychological phenomenon is called deindividuation. Deindividuation is even more pronounced when the person feels anonymous, or just a face in the crowd. When people know they will not be held accountable for their actions, they are more likely to join in a group's bad behavior.

In the 1970s several prominent studies on deindividuation were performed with school-aged children. On Halloween night, researchers set up an experiment in a neighborhood home. When children came to the door asking for candy, a researcher instructed them to take only one or two pieces from a bowl. The researcher then pretended to be called away, leaving the children alone with the candy bowl. Kids who were in groups were twice as likely to grab fistfuls of candy than those who came alone. And groups of children who wore masks were even more likely to steal.

Deindividuation can have far more serious consequences than stealing candy, of course. For example, deindividuation explains some of the behavior of the Ku Klux Klan, a white supremacist group responsible for brutally lynching thousands of African Americans in the mid-1800s through the 1950s. Klan members hid their identities under hoods and robes so they could act anonymously. This allowed members who might be hesitant to commit acts of such brutal violence to more easily act with the group.

when they see someone in emotional or physical pain. In fact, the empathy effect is so strong that people often share the emotions of characters in books and movies, crying when a character cries or wincing when a character is hurt.

Because of the human ability to understand and share the feelings of others, most people will not kill even if their rage response is triggered. Violence—especially premeditated or unprovoked violence—is not easy for people to commit. Yet violence among people who belong to different groups happens all the time. How are normally nonviolent people able to ignore their morals, shut off their empathy, and harm or kill other human beings?

In some cases the psychological process of dehumanization makes this possible. Dehumanization is the practice of attributing less-than-human characteristics to a group of people. According to philosophy professor David Livingstone Smith, "When people dehumanize others, they think of them as subhuman creatures or inanimate objects rather than human beings."[27] Examples from history include the era of American slavery, when people of European descent considered slaves of African descent to be less evolved and compared them to apes; the Rwandan genocide, when the Hutus characterized their victims, the Tutsis, as cockroaches and snakes; and the Holocaust, when the Nazi Party compared people of Jewish descent to rats. Dehumanization is almost always accompanied by oppression and violence. According to Smith, "Dehumanization is a way of overcoming our inhibitions against performing acts of violence for our own advantage. Conceiving of other people as rats, snakes, lice, dangerous predators, or beasts of burden, makes it much easier to treat them inhumanely."[28]

Dehumanization depends on the psychological tendency to see the human species as more evolved or superior to other living things. Many people believe that humans have an intangible essence inside that makes them human, and thus different from other animals. Belief in this intangible essence may have its roots in science (humans are the most evolved species) or in religion (humans are God's greatest achievement or are the only creatures with a soul). Dehumanization occurs when in-group members attribute human superiority to their group only, viewing out-group

The psychological process of dehumanization, or viewing a group of people as less than human, enabled German Nazis to commit unimaginable atrocities against other human beings in the 1930s and 1940s. This 1941 photograph shows a Nazi soldier executing a Jewish man in Ukraine.

members as not just different, but less human and therefore not entitled to the same legal protection or moral consideration.

Dehumanized groups are often viewed with intense hatred and are humiliated, tortured, and brutally murdered. Some psychologists believe this is because the idea that a human form contains a subhuman essence evokes deep emotions of fear and disgust. Dehumanization often involves characterizing victims as monstrous—evil entities in human form. For instance, in a 1942 propaganda booklet distributed by Himmler in Nazi Germany, Jewish people were described as follows: "Inside of this creature lies wild and unrestrained passions: an incessant need to destroy, filled with the most primitive desires, chaos, and coldhearted villainy. . . . These subhuman creatures dwell in the cesspools, and swamps, preferring a hell on earth, to the light of the sun."[29] In this passage Jewish people are described as demons—outwardly human, but inwardly subhuman and villainous. Smith notes that attributing monstrous or demonic characteristics to out-groups is commonly used to justify humiliation and torture.

Tolerance Is on the Rise

The human need to belong to a tribe and defend that tribe against outsiders has caused most of the violence that has plagued human history. Forces such as racism, nationalism, and religious fanaticism continue to drive tribal violence today. However, new technologies that promote interconnection and empathy have resulted in a celebration of diversity and a rise in tolerance in many cultures. Understanding the evolutionary roots of tribal psychology can only enhance this trend by encouraging people to question their mistrust and fear of those who are not like themselves.

CHAPTER 3

War

Nations almost always go to war to gain or protect territory and resources. But the individuals who fight those wars—the people who are ordered to kill, torture, rape, brutalize, and enslave their enemies—have much more complex psychological motives. Even though humans have a great capacity for violence, they are also hardwired for empathy. According to US Army historian S.L.A. Marshall, "The average and normally healthy individual . . . still has such an inner and usually unrealized resistance to killing a fellow man that he will not of his own volition take life if it is possible to turn away from that responsibility."[30]

How does a nation or group go to war when its members are so averse to killing? According to David Livingstone Smith, "Over the millennia, human beings developed methods for selectively disabling inhibitions against doing violence to others, so as to reap the advantages attendant upon war, genocide, and oppression."[31] These methods are used by armies and terrorist groups around the world to ensure that their soldiers will follow orders—to kill, torture, and terrorize.

Operant Conditioning

During World War II (1939–1945), Marshall conducted a series of post-combat interviews that revealed that three-quarters of US combat soldiers did not fire their weapons at the enemy. These soldiers would not shoot their attackers even to save their own lives or the lives of their friends. Instead, they either pretended to fire or deliberately aimed over the heads of the enemy.

When military experts realized what was happening, they began to change their training methods. By the Vietnam War (1955–1975), the new training methods had paid off. A full 95 percent of

Sudanese women fleeing the threat of genocide rest at a refugee camp in 2004. Fighters who commit crimes such as genocide usually have been subjected to psychological techniques that lower their innate aversion to taking a fellow human being's life.

soldiers had overcome their aversion to killing and were firing at the enemy in combat.

Natural resistance to killing was overcome through a psychological process called operant conditioning. According to psychology educator Kendra Cherry, "Operant conditioning relies on a fairly simple premise—actions that are followed by reinforcement will be strengthened and more likely to occur again in the future."[32] If this reinforcement happens over and over, the actions will eventually become automatic. For instance, a child who is praised for hanging up his or her jacket and scolded for dropping it on the floor will, after sufficient repetition, reflexively hang up the jacket. Operant conditioning is one of the main ways animals—including humans—learn.

This type of learning is extremely powerful because it allows humans to perform a complex set of behaviors automatically when they are under stress. According to Lieutenant Colonel Dave Grossman, author of *On Killing: The Psychological Cost of Learning to Kill in War and Society*, "When people are frightened or angry, they will do what they have been conditioned to do. In fire drills, children learn to file out of the school in orderly fashion. One day there is a real fire, and they are frightened out of their wits; but they do exactly what they have been conditioned to do, and it saves their lives."[33]

After World War II, military trainers began concentrating their training efforts on conditioning soldiers for combat. To do so, they began to make combat training as realistic as possible. Trainers replaced paper targets with simulated human figures that would behave realistically when shot. As sniper trainer Dale Dye describes, "I put clothes on these targets and polyurethane heads. I cut up a cabbage and poured catsup into it and put it back together. I said, 'When you look through that scope, I want you to see a head blowing up.'"[34] Soldiers began to practice in full gear in an environment that mimicked combat. Repetition became a key part of training.

Operant conditioning depends on there being a punishment or reward that gives learners immediate feedback on their performance. Since the concept of being rewarded for killing is distasteful even to career soldiers, rewards and punishments in operant conditioning for warfare are minimal. Poor performance might result in having to repeat the training, and good performance might earn the soldier a marksmanship badge or public recognition. Most of the reward came simply from hitting the target, which was often designed to fall over in a realistic fashion, providing the shooter with a sense of success.

According to Grossman, this new style of training created soldiers who were able to shoot instantly, without thought or hesitation. "Most modern infantry leaders understand that realistic training with immediate feedback to the soldier works," he explains, "and they know that it is essential for success and survival on the modern battlefield."[35]

Normalization

Operant conditioning is not the only technique used to turn military recruits into killers. In addition, violence can be made to seem unremarkable through a process called normalization. This process often happens naturally during wartime. Because soldiers are immersed in a military culture that views violence as a necessary and morally acceptable practice, the act of killing the enemy gradually becomes part of normal life.

The normalization of violence can also be a training technique. Soldiers are sometimes deliberately desensitized to violence by being exposed to it in stages. One horrific example of the normalization of violence occurs within armies or rebel groups that recruit children. For instance, according to researcher Mia Bloom, the Islamic State (IS) uses a specific process of normalization on children that has the effect of "slowly breaking down the boundaries, making something unnatural seem normal."[36] After befriend-

Video purported to be from the IS terrorist group shows young people being trained in the use of powerful weapons. The technique of desensitizing young people to violence by making it seem routine and normal produces individuals who are willing to kill others if they believe it is necessary and right to do so.

ing children by offering them candy and toys, IS fighters begin by showing children violent acts—first on video, and then live. Next they instruct the children to participate in violent acts by passing out weapons or leading prisoners to their death. The children are then trained in a brutal environment that causes them to bond closely with other child fighters. This process produces children who would lay down their lives for their friends and who believe that killing the enemy is normal and commonplace as well as necessary and right.

WORDS IN CONTEXT

normalization
A process by which constant and repeated exposure to an unfamiliar or distasteful practice causes it to seem commonplace or acceptable.

Theories of Good and Evil

Although IS and other terrorist groups train members to perform horrible acts of violence through operant conditioning or normalization, most national armies do not routinely give their combat soldiers this type of training. Yet soldiers have committed hideous acts of violence during warfare—and sometimes even seem to enjoy it. There are multiple instances of US soldiers torturing, brutalizing, or even murdering enemy soldiers and civilians in cold blood—behavior that cannot be explained by operant conditioning or normalization.

One of the most notable incidents of US soldiers engaging in this type of behavior occurred in the Abu Ghraib prison in Iraq. The prison was used by US forces at the beginning of the Iraq War (2003–2011) to hold captured enemy combatants, some of whom were interrogated by military intelligence. In April 2004 a US news program aired photographs of Abu Ghraib prisoners being physically and sexually abused, humiliated, and tortured. The pictures were taken by the prison guards themselves—military police who had no prison training. In many of the pictures, the guards posed with the tortured prisoners, smiling broadly at the camera or giving a thumbs-up sign.

Most people assume that this level of brutality is the fault of the soldiers, not the system. This is known as the dispositional theory of good and evil. As historian and scientist Michael Shermer explains, "The dispositional theory holds that evil is the result of bad dispositions in some people (a few bad apples)." In contrast, the situational theory of good and evil suggests that "evil is the product of corrupting circumstances (bad barrels that corrupt apples)," says Shermer. He sees behaviors like those at Abu Ghraib as a combination of the two. "We all have the capacity to commit evil deeds, but the expression of such acts very much depends on circumstances and conditions."[37]

The Lucifer Effect

Shermer's assessment of Abu Ghraib was based on a famous 1971 experiment conducted by psychologist Philip Zimbardo known as the Stanford prison experiment. Zimbardo recruited twenty-four male college students to spend two weeks in a makeshift prison playing the parts of either guards or prisoners (roles were assigned randomly). The "prisoners" were treated as realistically as possible: They were arrested at their homes by real policemen and were locked up in small cells in the basement of Stanford's psychology building, which was transformed into a prison for the experiment. The "guards" were given uniforms, clubs, and the authority to decide on their own how they would supervise the prisoners during the two-week experiment. Guards were not permitted to physically harm anyone, but otherwise they could behave as they liked.

On the second day of the experiment, the prisoners rebelled. As Zimbardo explains, it was at that point that the guards began abusing the prisoners:

> All 12 guards came in, and they crushed the rebellion. At that point, the guards said, "These are dangerous prisoners. We have to show who is in charge, who is the boss." That changed everything. That's when it became a prison. No one used the word "experiment" again. The guards used physical force—stripped the prisoners naked, put them in chains, put them in solitary confinement. There was actually fighting. The guards used psychological force to make prisoners feel helpless and hopeless.[38]

The behavior of the guards became so cruel and the prisoners became so demoralized that Zimbardo called off the experiment after only six days.

In the years since, the Stanford prison experiment has become a staple of psychology textbooks as an explanation of how a situation can cause good people to do bad things. "We knew these students were good apples," Zimbardo says. "Yet within days, the guards were transformed into sadistic thugs and the prisoners were emotionally broken." As he writes in *The Lucifer Effect: Understanding How Good People Turn Evil*, "If you put good apples in a bad situation, you'll get bad apples."[39]

When the soldiers who had been involved in Abu Ghraib were brought to trial, Zimbardo was called on as an expert witness. He saw many similarities between the brutal torture that occurred at the Abu Ghraib prison and the behavior of the guards in his

Modern Warfare

Brandon Bryant was a drone pilot for the US Air Force between 2005 and 2011. In one of his missions, he tracked a small group of suspected insurgents in Afghanistan for several hours until they fell asleep for the night, then launched a missile at the group, killing them all. Bryant was shaken by the mission, which he carried out from a base outside of Las Vegas, Nevada. "We waited for those men to settle down in their beds and then we killed them in their sleep," he said. "That was cowardly murder."

Bryant is part of a new way to wage war. Military drones—pilotless, radio-controlled aircraft that can be operated from thousands of miles away—allow soldiers to kill by remote control. Michael Haas, another drone pilot, says the experience is extremely disturbing. "You start to do these psychological gymnastics to make it easier to do what you have to do—they deserved it, they chose their side. You had to kill part of your conscience to keep doing your job every day—and ignore those voices telling you this wasn't right."

Quoted in Ed Pilkington, "Life as a Drone Operator," *Guardian* (Manchester), November 19, 2015. www.theguardian.com.

experiment. Even though Zimbardo's guards were not physically brutal, they, like the Abu Ghraib guards, humiliated the prisoners for their own amusement. Zimbardo explains, "As the boredom of their job increased, they [the guards in the experiment] began using the prisoners as their playthings, devising ever more humiliating and degrading games for them to play. Over time, these amusements took a sexual turn, such as having the prisoners simulate sodomy on each other."[40] This is similar to what happened at Abu Ghraib. The soldiers not only tortured and abused the prisoners, they devised increasingly bizarre ways to humiliate them sexually.

Zimbardo believes that it was the situation at Abu Ghraib that caused the soldiers to abuse their prisoners. The Abu Ghraib prison had been used for torture by the Iraqi government before it was commandeered by the US military. It was a horrible environment, filthy and broken down, with no running water or toilets. It was also under constant enemy attack. The soldiers worked twelve-hour shifts and had been stationed inside the prison for more than a month without a break. They were also responsible for preparing the prisoners for interrogation. The US government had authorized torture to be used in these interrogations, which the soldiers knew. Their superiors did not order or officially condone the abuses, but they turned a blind eye to them and instead praised the soldiers for their work.

These conditions created a situation where soldiers with normal and stable psychological profiles committed horrendous acts. Still, Zimbardo believes they should be held responsible for their actions. At the same time, he also believes that the soldiers' superiors, as well as the system that condoned torture, should assume most of the blame.

The Power of Purpose

Most young men and women do not join an army because they want to kill, torture, and brutalize others. They choose to serve in the military because they have a strong belief in the ideology of their in-group. The ideological goal of war may be specific (to win independence from a dictator) or general (to support one's nation). The ideology may also be based on religious beliefs. War allows

An American soldier adjusts his rifle sight in Afghanistan. Despite the bloodshed that warfare inevitably produces, most recruits volunteer for the military for ideological reasons and not because they want to kill or otherwise harm others.

people to actively fight for the ideologies of their in-groups, which most cultures view as a noble and honorable pursuit.

Warfare also gives young people a mission. "War gives you a tremendous sense of purpose and energy," explains documentary filmmaker Sebastian Junger. "Out there, there is a very strong sense of brotherhood, there's a lot of adrenalin."[41] In fact, for many young men and women, warfare has some positive psychological aspects. As psychologist Steve Taylor explains, war "makes people feel more alive, more alert and awake. . . . It supplies meaning and purpose, transcending the monotony of everyday life. . . . Warfare also enables the expression of higher human qualities which often lie dormant in ordinary life, such as discipline, courage, unselfishness and self-sacrifice."[42]

Strong ideological beliefs coupled with a yearning for a sense of purpose can drive young people to join a military group even if it commits atrocities against out-groups. An example of this is

The Spoils of War

Terrorist organizations often recruit poor young men who do not have any way to earn enough money to attract a wife or support their families. Taru Daniel, a twenty-three-year-old Nigerian man who escaped a raid by the Islamic terrorist group Boko Haram, understands why other young Nigerian men join Boko Haram. "We have nothing," he explains. "That is why they join. For some small, small money. For a wife."

The desire for sex and the need to procreate is an extremely strong biological and psychological drive in humans—especially in males in their late teens and twenties. "Any creature that is recognizably on track towards complete reproductive failure must somehow expend effort, often at risk of death, to try to improve its present life trajectory," explain psychologists Martin Daly and Margo Wilson. For this reason, terrorist organizations even use the promise of rape to recruit these men. This draw is even more powerful if raping women can be justified by religious ideology. For instance, Muslim men are not permitted to have sex outside of marriage. However, IS uses religion to authorize its soldiers to buy, sell, and rape non-Muslim women. As journalist Rukmini Callimachi explains, IS uses religious texts "to not only justify violence, but also to elevate and celebrate each sexual assault as spiritually beneficial, even virtuous."

Quoted in *Economist*, "Of Men and Mayhem," January 23, 2016. www.economist.com.

Quoted in John Sexton, "Captured ISIS Solider: Rape of Yazidi Women 'Is Normal,'" Hot Air, February 17, 2017. http://hotair.com.

the recruiting success of IS, which offers young people a chance to be part of a war that has the goal of reestablishing the Islamic caliphate, or religious society ruled by a holy leader. "Recruits are driven by this passionate need to right some perceived wrong, to address some sort of injustice, to restore honor to those from whom it's been taken," explains psychologist John Horgan. He says that IS is particularly effective at "offering an opportunity for people to feel powerful. They're making disillusioned, disaffected radicals feel like they're doing something truly meaningful with their lives."[43] That power is expressed by complete dominion over all nonbelievers, who are slaughtered or enslaved.

According to Horgan, once recruits join an organization like IS, they are gradually desensitized to violence, which is eventually normalized. This can be a lengthy process, and recruits can become disillusioned when they are faced with the extreme brutality these groups perpetrate on civilians. Horgan explains that recruits often "take refuge in ideology when faced with the reality of doing something horrific."[44] In this case the ideology of IS includes the belief that violence against nonbelievers is not only necessary, but the work of God. For IS, war is a holy purpose.

War Is in Decline

War brings out the worst in humans. People have been waging war for at least ten thousand years, starting when hunter-gatherers attacked and brutally killed members of neighboring tribes. Today sophisticated psychological conditioning coupled with the power of the group can lead people to commit horrible acts of violence against each other. However, warfare seems to be on the decline. The past several decades have been the most peaceful in recent history, and fewer people are being killed in battle than ever before. As people improve their understanding of how they can be psychologically manipulated to hate, fear, and kill members of opposing groups, they may become more likely to resist the forces that drive humanity to war.

CHAPTER 4

Psychological Effects of Violence

When Christine Suhan was a young woman, she was violently raped. Thirteen years later she still experiences the effects that violent encounter had on her brain. For instance, during an intimate moment with her husband, Suhan suddenly felt as though she was again being sexually assaulted. "I felt trapped. I couldn't breathe. In a split second my body went from passionate love-making to fight-or-flight mode," she writes. "I ripped my husband's arms off of me, threw a few automatic punches and jumped backward."[45]

Suhan suffers from post-traumatic stress disorder (PTSD), a brain-based disorder caused by physical and emotional trauma. PTSD causes changes in the brain that make it relive a traumatic event again and again. "My brain can't differentiate the past from the present and mistakenly thinks that I am re-living the trauma," Suhan explains. "I have to give my brain stem time . . . before it can realize that 13 years have passed since the rape and I'm in a safe place with a safe person."[46]

Psychological Effects of Emotional Trauma

When a person is under threat, his or her brain automatically activates the fight-or-flight response. Sometimes such an experience does not have a lasting emotional effect. But if the experience is disturbing or frightening enough, a person will experience emotional trauma, which *Merriam-Webster* defines as "a disordered psychic or behavioral state resulting from severe mental or emotional stress or physical injury."[47] Emotional trauma often involves feelings of fear, anger, guilt, and sadness, which can linger long after the traumatic event has passed. It can also be accompanied by a host of painful psychological aftereffects, including anxiety, hypervigilance (being on high alert to danger), insomnia, depression, or bouts of aggression.

In most people symptoms of emotional trauma gradually diminish as the memory of the traumatic event fades. Eventually, the individual is able to return to normal psychological functioning. However, in some people the effects of emotional trauma do not fade. When this happens, a person may be diagnosed with PTSD.

The brain of a person with PTSD—specifically, the areas involved in threat detection and memory—has been damaged by the traumatic event. People with PTSD often describe their traumatic memories as flashbacks: sudden, vivid recollections of past events that evoke intense emotional responses. When a traumatic flashback is triggered, the brains of people with PTSD respond as though the event is happening in real time. Their flight-or-flight response activates, causing their heart rate to speed up, their bodies to flood with the substances adrenaline and cortisol, and their perceptions of reality to alter. This experience can be so terrifying that the PTSD sufferer will try to avoid thinking about the event at all. "Usually victims try to avoid people, objects, and situations that remind them of their hurtful experiences," says psychologist Viatcheslav Wlassoff. "This behavior is debilitating and prevents them from living their lives meaningfully."[48]

Many people with PTSD are never able to turn off their fight-or-flight response. "Frightened and traumatized, they are almost always on edge,"[49] explains Wlassoff. They remain on high alert, experiencing constant fear and paranoia. They have trouble managing their emotions and often act inappropriately with others. They may lash out or retreat from the world, and they sometimes try to dull their feelings of intense anxiety with drugs or alcohol.

Soldiers who return from battle with PTSD have a higher risk of becoming violent when triggered. This is because they have

> ## WORDS IN CONTEXT
>
> **hypervigilance**
> An enhanced state of alertness and sensitivity to real or imagined threats.

Experiencing a traumatic event can produce post-traumatic stress disorder, or PTSD. Sufferers of the disorder experience flashbacks to the event that make it seem as if it is taking place again in the present moment.

been trained, through operant conditioning, to immediately respond to threat with violence. "When one is exposed to war-zone trauma and combat trauma, they are going to be more likely to assume the worst and assume people are trying to do harm to them—and more likely to respond to that with aggressions,"[50] explains Dr. Casey Taft, who researches PTSD as part of his work with the US Department of Veterans Affairs. According to Taft, veterans with PTSD are three times more likely to be violent than civilians suffering from the disorder. This violence often affects those closest to the veteran—their spouses and children. For instance, as the wife of a US veteran with PTSD recounted on National Public Radio, when she tried to wake her husband from a nightmare, "He was shrieking with his eyes open. And I went to shake him. He grabbed my wrist and twisted it. . . . I know my wrist was broken."[51]

As evidenced by PTSD, experiencing emotional trauma can have profound effects on the brain. The most significant changes occur in the hippocampus—a small structure near the center of the brain that is involved in memory formation and retrieval. The hippocampus also allows people to tell the difference between memories that were formed long ago and memories that were formed recently. The hippocampus is linked with the amygdala, the nearby structure that controls the fight-or-flight response. When people encounter a dangerous situation, the amygdala and the hippocampus work together to determine if the situation is life threatening based on stored knowledge and memories.

> **WORDS IN CONTEXT**
>
> **trauma**
> An experience that is deeply distressing or disturbing to the psyche, often with lasting psychological effect.

Neuroimaging studies on people with PTSD have revealed that they have a smaller hippocampus, which means that there are fewer neural connections formed within the structure and fewer links to outside structures like the amygdala. This means that the functioning of the hippocampus is impaired. Because of this, when a memory of a traumatic event is triggered, the amygdala does not get the message that the event happened in the past. Instead, the fight-or-flight response is triggered, and the individual goes on high alert. While he or she may understand that the traumatic event happened in the past, his or her body still reacts as if there is immediate danger.

People with PTSD also have increased activity in their amygdala. This causes ongoing anxiety, panic, and extreme stress—especially when something triggers a memory of the traumatic event. Their hyperactive amygdala can also cause them to overreact to other upsetting or stressful situations. As Wlassoff explains, "These people exhibit fear and stress responses . . . when they are simply shown photographs of people exhibiting fear."[52]

This effect is compounded by another brain change—a reduction in functioning of the part of the prefrontal cortex that allows

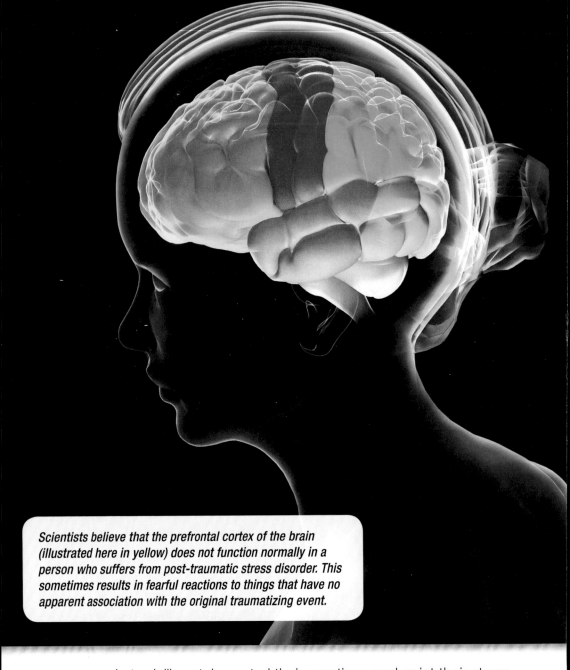

Scientists believe that the prefrontal cortex of the brain (illustrated here in yellow) does not function normally in a person who suffers from post-traumatic stress disorder. This sometimes results in fearful reactions to things that have no apparent association with the original traumatizing event.

people to deliberately control their emotions and quiet their stress responses. Wlassoff says that reduced functioning in the prefrontal cortex "explains why people suffering from PTSD tend to exhibit fear, anxiety, and extreme stress responses even when faced with stimuli not connected—or only remotely connected—to their experiences from the past."[53]

Risk Factors for PTSD

Scientists do not completely understand why some traumatic events cause PTSD and some do not or why some people are more vulnerable to the disorder than others. Because PTSD changes the way the brain processes stress, scientists believe that risk factors can include prior trauma, elevated stress levels, or mental health disorders (like depression or anxiety) that make people more vulnerable to stress. The brains of people with these risk factors may already have been changed by stress, which then makes it harder for the brain to process trauma. Researchers have found that women are twice as likely as men to develop PTSD. This may be because, due to generally possessing less muscle mass, women often perceive traumatic events as more physically dangerous. In addition, people who have a family history of PTSD seem to be more vulnerable to the disorder. Scientists still do not know if this is because PTSD sufferers do not teach their children healthy ways of dealing with stress or if the vulnerability is genetic. In general, scientists believe that all of these risk factors are cumulative.

People who have good coping skills and strong support networks seem to be protected somewhat from PTSD. Post-trauma therapy also seems to help. Therapists can assess whether a trauma victim is processing the memory of the trauma in a healthy way. They can help victims who are either fixating on the memory or attempting to block it—common features of PTSD. They can also help those who blame themselves for the trauma or are otherwise experiencing shame, both of which seem to be risk factors for PTSD. Scientists are also developing a screening tool that will identify some of these risk factors in trauma victims so that those who are at risk of developing PTSD can get help quickly.

The Brain's Response to Torture

In addition to PTSD, traumatic violence such as torture can create other changes to the brain. Torture is defined as inflicting severe pain on another person. That pain can be physical, emotional, or a combination of the two. People torture for a variety of reasons: to gain information in an interrogation; to establish dominance and control over another person (as may happen in a domestic abuse situation); or in a sadistic individual, for sport or pleasure. Torture can induce a state known as learned helplessness. Learned helplessness occurs when people learn, through trial and error, that they cannot help themselves. People in a state of learned helplessness are overcome by a sense of powerlessness and apathy, and they often will not try to help themselves even if it becomes possible. For instance, a torture victim in a state of learned helplessness may not try to escape, even if the opportunity presents itself.

After the terror attacks in New York City and Washington, DC, on September 11, 2001, the CIA began using torture in its interrogation of suspected terrorists based on the theory of learned helplessness. According to a Senate Intelligence Committee report quoted in the *New Yorker*, CIA psychologists believed that "detainees might become passive and depressed in response to adverse or uncontrollable events, and would thus cooperate and provide information."[54] This was the reasoning behind the torture inflicted on the prisoners in the Abu Ghraib prison in Iraq. If people were interrogated in a state of learned helplessness, military psychologists reasoned, they would be more likely to divulge information.

Psychologists now know that inducing a state of learned helplessness through repeated physical and emotional trauma has a profoundly negative effect on the memory centers of the brain. "Memories are fragile, subject to revision and loss," explains Shane O'Mara, director of the Trinity College Institute of Neuroscience and an expert on the psychological effects of torture. "Severe stressors of the type used during torture . . . disrupt the consolidation of memory, and erode one's ability to retrieve memories—even of simple, straightforward, fact-based information."[55] In other words, just as it does in people with PTSD, severe or prolonged trauma disrupts the brain's ability to process memories. A person who is under severe stress cannot reliably retrieve memories, nor can he or she tell if those memories are accurate. Ironically, then, though torture is often committed to obtain information, any information obtained will most likely be unreliable. As O'Mara asserts, "Torture, as an interrogational tactic, has been proven to be a complete and utter failure."[56]

The Effects of Violence on Children

Children are particularly vulnerable to violence-induced emotional trauma—especially when that violence occurs within the home. Child abuse is all too common in the United States. According to the Centers for Disease Control and Prevention, over seven

New Therapies for PTSD

Recent studies have found that the ability to control attention and focus may protect people from developing PTSD. A 2014 study published in *European Psychiatry* compared functional magnetic resonance imaging (fMRI) brain scans of Dutch veterans who suffered from PTSD with those who did not. The study found that veterans without PTSD had stronger connections in the medial prefrontal cortex—the part of the brain behind the forehead involved in controlling attention and regulating emotional responses. This means that the veterans who did not have PTSD were better able to control what they thought about. The researchers believe that increasing neural connections in the medial prefrontal cortex—in other words, building attention skills—might protect people from developing PTSD. It might also help people already suffering from the disorder recover.

Meditation, which increases neural connections and builds attention, is showing a great deal of promise in treating PTSD. A 2016 study published in *Military Medicine* compared soldiers with PTSD who practiced transcendental meditation to solders who did not. After one month 83.7 percent of the meditators were able to reduce or stop their medication for PTSD, compared to only 59.4 percent of the control group. In addition, only 10.9 percent of the meditators needed to increase their medication, compared to 40.5 percent of the control group. As the study's lead author, physiologist Vernon Barnes, explains, "Regular practice of Transcendental Meditation provides a habit of calming down and healing the brain."

Quoted in Christopher Bergland, "Meditation Reduces Post-Traumatic Stress Disorder Symptoms," *The Athlete's Way* (blog), *Psychology Today*, January 13, 2016. www.psychologytoday.com.

hundred thousand children were abused in 2014, and experts estimate that one in four children will experience abuse at some point during their childhood. Domestic partner violence is also prevalent in families with children; studies estimate that 3.3 million to 10 million children witness violence between their parents or caretakers each year.

Because children have a deep need to rely on their parents, young children rarely blame their parents for abuse. Instead, they tend to blame themselves. According to psychotherapist Beverly Engel, "In essence [children who are abused are] saying to themselves, 'My mother is treating me like this because I've been bad,' or, 'I am being neglected because I am unlovable.'"[57] This results in pervasive feelings of shame in abused children, which can cause them to develop mental disorders like depression and

Children who are victims of abuse at home are particularly vulnerable to violence-induced emotional trauma. Lacking the reasoning ability of adults, such children tend to blame their abuse on their own behavior rather than that of their abusers.

anxiety. It can also cause lasting self-esteem issues that can interfere with quality of life and the ability to form healthy adult relationships.

Violence in the home can also disrupt a child's psychological and social development. In young children healthy brain development depends on healthy interactions with adults in a safe and secure environment. Children are born with the need to bond with a parent or caregiver, a process that psychologists call attachment. According to attachment theory, this first bond allows a child's brain to make the neural connections necessary for healthy growth and development. In addition, when children are confident that a parent can provide safety and security, they are able to attach to other people and create new relationships—with siblings, friends, teachers, and other adults. However, if a parent cannot be relied on to keep the child safe—either because the parent is abusing the child or there is violence between adults in the home—the child cannot form other healthy relationships and is at risk of developing emotional and behavioral problems that can last a lifetime.

Children who are severely neglected or traumatized by abuse early in life are also at risk of developing reactive attachment disorder (RAD). Children with RAD stop looking to adults for comfort and have profound difficulties creating relationships with others. Some children with RAD never develop the ability to empathize with others. According to the Institute for Attachment and Child Development, some characteristics of RAD include having a lack of remorse, conscience, or compassion for others; lying, stealing, and cheating; and destructive and cruel behavior.

Children and PTSD

Children in violent environments also are at risk of developing PTSD. According to social worker Lauren Isaac, these children "develop the sense that . . . [they are] in constant danger; also known as the 'fight-or-flight' response; meaning that they will be in a consistent state of hyper vigilance."[58] These children often have sleep and appetite disturbances, constant fatigue, difficulty concentrating, reduced cognitive function, and chronic physical pain.

Children with PTSD frequently behave like children who are suffering from attention-deficit/hyperactivity disorder (ADHD)—they have poor impulse control, display aggressiveness and hyperactivity, and are unable to interact appropriately with other children. These children are often misdiagnosed and treated for ADHD with stimulant medications, which does not address the problems of ongoing physical abuse and emotional trauma in the home.

Normalizing Violence

Social learning theory posits that children learn norms of behavior by observing their parents and other adults. The theory holds that learning is a cognitive process that occurs in a social context. In other words, children are able to learn simply by observing another person's actions or behaviors. If children witness violence in the home, they learn that violence is normal and acceptable, and they will imitate the violent behavior.

Social learning theory was developed by psychologist Albert Bandura in the early 1960s. The theory was demonstrated in a series of psychological experiments on children known as the Bobo doll experiments. Bandura recruited children between the ages of three and six and placed them individually in a playroom with an adult. Some of the adults violently attacked one of the toys in the playroom called a Bobo doll—a large clown-shaped doll weighted on the bottom that could be used as a punching bag. The adult modeled violent behavior by punching the doll, hitting it with a mallet, kicking it around the room, and shouting at it. Next, all the children were placed in a room with desirable toys that they were not allowed to play with, with the aim of elevating their frustration levels. Finally, they were each placed in a room alone with another set of toys and a Bobo doll.

As Bandura predicted, the children who had witnessed the adult behaving violently toward the Bobo doll imitated the adult's behavior almost exactly. They punched, kicked, and yelled at the Bobo doll, expressing far more aggressive behavior than the control group, who had also become frustrated by not being allowed to play with toys but had not witnessed any violence toward the doll. As psychology educator Kendra Cherry explains, "According

Depression Research Used for Developing Torture

One of the most famous experiments in learned helplessness was conducted by psychologist Martin Seligman in 1967. Seligman wanted to help people who suffered from depression regain their motivation. To explore this subject, he created an experiment in learned helplessness. Seligman placed dogs in an enclosure and randomly delivered electric shocks to the floor of their cages. Some of the dogs could stop the shocks by pushing a lever, but some could not. He then placed the dogs in enclosures where they could move away from the shocks. The dogs who had been able to stop the shocks previously figured out how to avoid the new shocks. However, the dogs who had learned that they were helpless made no effort to avoid the new shocks; they simply lay down and whined. Next, Seligman showed the helpless dogs how to avoid the shocks by moving their limbs. After a few repetitions, the dogs were no longer apathetic and avoided the shocks on their own. Seligman concluded that the dogs did not try to escape the shocks because they expected to fail, but once they were shown they could succeed, they regained their motivation.

Seligman's learned helplessness experiments were used to develop the CIA torture program. When this was revealed in 2014, Seligman was stunned. He said he was "grieved that good science, which has helped many people overcome depression, may have been used for such a bad purpose as torture."

Quoted in Maria Konnikova, "Trying to Cure Depression, but Inspiring Torture," *New Yorker*, January 14, 2015. www.newyorker.com.

to Bandura, the violent behavior of the adult models toward the dolls led children to believe that such actions were acceptable. He also suggested that as a result, children may be more inclined to respond to frustration with aggression in the future."[59]

Bandura's results, which have been confirmed by similar studies, explain why children from violent homes tend to be far more aggressive than other children. These children also have a harder time reading social cues when interacting with their peers. "Children who are exposed to higher aggression in the household between parents are having more difficulty reading the signals or the signs of others' negative emotions accurately," explains psychologist C. Cybele Raver. "So if they're coming down the stairs at school and another child bumps into them, they may respond in an aggressive way."[60]

The Cyclical Nature of Violence

Some psychologists have characterized violence as a disease—a contagion that is passed from aggressor to victim. As victims of violence deal with the psychological damage caused by their experiences, they can lash out violently at their loved ones. Children who witness or are victims of violence learn that it is an acceptable response to conflict and become violent themselves, often going on to abuse their own spouse or children. Only by putting an end to the cycle of violence can society hope to prevent the damage violence does to the brain.

CHAPTER 5

Abnormal Psychology and Violence

Most mentally ill people are not violent, and most violence is not caused by mental illness or abnormal psychology. However, violence in the mentally ill does happen, though mentally ill people are much more likely to harm themselves than to harm others. Violence toward others by the mentally ill is more likely to occur when a person is in a psychotic state. In addition, some mental conditions correlate strongly with violent behavior. People with these conditions have in common a lack of empathy—a trait that makes it much more likely that they will harm others.

Mental Illness and Violence

On June 12, 2016, Omar Mateen entered the Pulse nightclub in Orlando, Florida, and opened fire on the packed crowd inside. Mateen murdered forty-nine people and injured fifty-three more before he was killed by police. While he had never been diagnosed with a mental illness, several media sources cited his wife's description of his unstable behavior as evidence that a mental disorder had driven Mateen to kill. However, according to psychologist Laura Hayes, it was not mental illness that turned him into a killer. Mateen was already a violent person, prone to physical violence and bouts of rage. "There is no form of mental illness that predicts murderous behavior," Hayes explains. "Violence is not a product of mental illness. Violent crimes are committed by violent people, people who are unable to manage their anger."[61]

According to a 2016 study published in the journal *Health Affairs*, only about 4 percent of violence in the United States is

Visitors view a memorial that sprang up in the wake of the June 12, 2016, attack on the Pulse nightclub in Orlando, Florida, that killed forty-nine people and injured another fifty-three. Although the shooting was widely attributed to mental illness on the part of the culprit, experts say that violence is not usually a product of mental illness.

caused by mental illness. As psychologist Jillian Peterson explains, "The vast majority of people with mental illness are not violent, not criminal and not dangerous."[62] Those who do become violent are usually in the throes of psychosis. However, psychosis by itself does not cause violent behavior. According to a 2013 study published in *JAMA Psychiatry*, psychosis is only associated with violence when it is combined with rage. As the study's authors write, "Anger due to delusion is a key factor that explains the relationship between violence and acute psychosis."[63]

Psychosis and Delusional Thinking

People who are psychotic often suffer from delusional thinking. A delusion is a firmly held belief that is not or cannot be true. People who have delusions insist that their beliefs are true, despite clear proof that they are false. Delusional thinking is not evidence of a mental illness—many mentally healthy people believe things that have been proved false. But delusions can be a symptom of mental illness, especially when they are accompanied by disordered thinking.

Delusions and psychosis can manifest in a variety of mental disorders, including schizophrenia, depression, bipolar disorder, and dementia. The most serious of these mental illnesses is schizophrenia, a disease in which one's thought processes and emotions become highly disordered and fragmented, leading to a blurring of fantasy and reality. Schizophrenia is characterized by persistent hallucinations, delusional thinking that is sometimes grandiose or paranoid in nature, and—in the acute stage—psychosis, which can sometimes lead to violence.

While there are several types of schizophrenia, the type most commonly associated with violence is paranoid schizophrenia. People suffering from paranoid schizophrenia experience intense anxiety, suspicion, and fear of others. Their thinking can become disordered and illogical, leading to the belief that they are being persecuted in some way. These delusional beliefs are accompanied by hallucinations that commonly take the form of voices. To a person suffering from schizophrenia, these voices are indistinguishable from real speech. Neuroscientists believe that these hallucinations are caused by a malfunction in the auditory processing function of the brain. Because of this malfunction, schizophrenics do not recognize that these voices are being generated by their own thoughts, which makes them prone to delusional thinking. Some common delusions among

> ### WORDS IN CONTEXT
>
> **psychosis**
> A mental state in which one's thoughts and feelings are so disrupted and disorganized that a person is no longer in touch with reality.

Paranoia

Paranoia is a thought process that revolves around persecutory thinking—the idea that people are attempting to harm the paranoid person. It often is accompanied by hypervigilance, anxiety, and fear. Paranoia is thought to be closely connected to the fight-or-flight response, which is why it can lead to rage and violence.

Paranoid people often demonstrate what psychologists call attribution bias. People who exhibit attribution bias are not interpreting the motivations of others correctly. For instance, if a woman believes she has been fired because her boss hates her—when in fact she was fired because she was making errors on the job—she is exhibiting attribution bias. Most people exhibit attribution bias at some point in their lives, but when that bias is accompanied by fear, anxiety, depression, and a need to isolate and protect oneself, paranoia is most likely the cause.

Paranoia is not, in itself, an official mental disorder. But because it is linked with the fight-or-flight response and aggressive behavior, it can be a dangerous feature of mental illnesses or personality disorders that are associated with violence. For example, psychiatrist Phillip J. Resnick describes a man with paranoid schizophrenia who developed a delusion that there was a conspiracy to kill him. When his wife took him to the hospital to be evaluated, he concluded she was part of the conspiracy and stabbed her to death. Because he was paranoid, the man misunderstood his wife's motivations and responded with deadly violence.

people who suffer from auditory hallucinations are that their minds are being invaded by aliens, they are in contact with God or other supernatural beings, or that the government is employing mind control technology to control them.

People with schizophrenia are about four times more likely to be violent than the general population. In most cases violence among schizophrenics is directed toward family members and is complicated by substance abuse. However, the idea that schizophrenics are prone to violent killing sprees is a myth. Researchers have estimated that the chance of being killed by a stranger suffering from schizophrenia is about 1 in 14 million. Medication can reduce hallucinations and allow a person with schizophrenia to think more clearly—which typically eliminates any violent impulses.

Delusions and Violence

When people with schizophrenia or other mental illnesses become violent, it is usually the case that they are operating under a paranoid delusion. They are convinced that they—or the people they love—are in immediate danger. "Persecutory delusions are more likely to lead to homicide than any other psychiatric symptom,"[64] explains psychiatrist Phillip J. Resnick. Resnick, who has performed more than one hundred sanity evaluations on people charged with murder, believes that those suffering from paranoid delusions kill for four reasons: in self-defense, in defense of one's manhood (often brought on by homophobia), in defense of one's children, or in defense of the world. For instance, one man Resnick evaluated believed that his former high school football coach had the team rape him each night while he slept, so he shot the

People with serious mental illnesses such as schizophrenia may turn to violence under a delusion that they are protecting themselves or their loved ones from immediate danger. Such people have a great deal of difficulty distinguishing reality from fantasy.

coach (defense of one's manhood). In another example, a deeply religious woman believed her children were in danger from child pornographers, so to save their souls she killed them (defense of one's children).

People who kill in these circumstances are often experiencing the fight-or-flight response. And because they are not interpreting reality accurately, they believe an extreme fight response is necessary. "Someone trapped inside a delusion, complete with its own illusory sights, smells, and sounds, can't tell reality from fantasy," explains psychologist Betsy Seifter. "Someone who can't trust his own senses and is in [a] state of internal chaos and fear . . . can't tell the good guys from the bad guys."[65] The psychotic state—particularly when combined with the fight-or-flight response—also disrupts thinking processes in the prefrontal cortex, which is responsible for keeping violent impulses in check. This makes it more likely that a psychotic person will react to a perceived threat with rage and violence.

The Role of Empathy

There is another psychological condition that is linked with violence—a lack of empathy. Empathy is often associated with compassion, which literally means "to suffer together." When a person feels compassion, he or she is motivated to help relieve the suffering of others. Empathy often leads to compassion, but not always. Sometimes sharing another's emotions can be so painful that a person will turn away rather than attempt to help.

People who have low empathy have a limited ability to feel what others feel. They may be able to understand how another person is feeling, but they do not feel the corresponding emotions. This puts people with low empathy at a distinct disadvantage when it comes to social relationships. Human connections are rooted in the ability to empathize—to connect through the shared feelings of love and friendship. Because people with low empathy are often unaffected by the emotional state of others, they have little motivation to behave with kindness and compassion. They also often cannot offer the understanding that people tend to desire most in relationships.

Mirror Neurons

Scientists have discovered that empathy is associated with specialized cells in the brain called mirror neurons. When someone observes emotions in another person, the mirror neurons in the observer's brain generate—or mirror—the emotions that are observed. For instance, human infants who observe fear on their mothers' faces will react with fear and distress, even though they have no conscious understanding of danger.

Mirror neurons are why humans often have a strong emotional reaction when they see another person in pain and why behaviors such as laughter or yawning are contagious. According to psychiatrist Amy Banks, "There have been studies that look at emotions in human beings such as disgust, shame, happiness, where the exact same areas of the brain light up in the listener who is reading the feelings of the person talking. We are, literally, hardwired to connect."

Some researchers believe that people with psychopathy and other disorders of low empathy may have dysfunctional mirror neuron systems. Other scientists believe that psychopaths are simply able to turn their empathy system on or off on demand, activating their mirror neurons at will. This allows them to harm others without regret.

Quoted in Rebecca Eanes, "Wired to Connect—Discipline Shouldn't Hurt," Positive Parenting: Toddlers & Beyond, July 23, 2014. www.positive-parents.org.

People with low or no empathy are not mentally ill, and there is no evidence that people with low empathy are more prone to violence. However, when low empathy is paired with a disregard for others—as it is in certain personality disorders—the risk of violent behavior becomes much more pronounced.

Personality Disorders and Low Empathy

Personality disorders are not mental illnesses. Instead, they are rigid and maladaptive behaviors that interfere with well-being and happiness. People with personality disorders usually have a hard time forming positive relationships or interacting with others in a productive way. People with these disorders rarely recognize that their personality traits are at the root of their problems, and therefore they almost never seek treatment. At the same time, most psychologists do not believe that personality disorders can be treated effectively, because they are part of the individual's essential character. Although all people with personality disorders have difficulties understanding and connecting with others, there are three personality disorders that are specifically associated with low empathy: narcissistic personality disorder, borderline personality disorder, and antisocial personality disorder.

People with narcissistic personality disorder have a sense of entitlement, a need to be admired, and an unshakable belief in their own importance. Many have a certain amount of social charisma that can make them the center of attention. However, they also lie compulsively to make themselves seem more important, and they will exploit others to help themselves. They also tend to be so self-absorbed that they lack awareness of the feelings of others and therefore have difficulty with close personal relationships. It is not clear if people with narcissistic personality disorder lack the ability to be empathetic or if they simply choose to disengage from any empathetic response that does not benefit them.

Narcissists can also be prone to fits of rage. As psychiatrist Neel Burton describes, "If he [a narcissist] feels obstructed or ridiculed, he can fly into a fit of destructive anger and revenge. Such a reaction is sometimes called 'narcissistic rage', and can have disastrous consequences for all those involved."[66]

People with borderline personality disorder have a poorly formed sense of self and an intense fear of abandonment. The disorder is marked by heightened emotions, mood swings, and paranoid and delusional thinking. Like narcissists, borderlines can be charismatic. They tend to crave relationships and are constantly seeking them out; however, their manipulative and impulsive behavior usually guarantees that any relationships they form are chaotic and short lived. They are also prone to fits of rage over perceived slights or betrayals, which can lead to violent behavior.

Through fMRI imaging, scientists have recently discovered that borderlines have reduced empathy activity in the brain. Scientists believe that this is one reason why borderlines have such difficulty with relationships. According to psychologist Brian Haas, the lead author of one such study, "This reduced activation [of empathy] may suggest that people with more BPD [borderline personality disorder] traits have a more difficult time understanding and/ or predicting how others feel."[67] A lack of empathy also explains why they are more likely to harm others. In addition, up to 50 percent of borderlines also have features of narcissistic and/or antisocial personality disorder, both of which are associated with violent behavior.

Of all officially recognized mental illnesses and personality disorders, antisocial personality disorder is most closely correlated with violence. People with an antisocial personality have a lack of empathy combined with a callous disregard for the feelings and rights of others. They ignore rules and laws, are impulsive, tend to be violent, and do not feel guilt over their actions. They also tend to be irritable and aggressive, and they often fail to learn from experience. About 40 percent to 70 percent of all prison inmates exhibit features of antisocial personality disorder, even though only about 1 percent to 3 percent of the general population have the disorder.

> **WORDS IN CONTEXT**
>
> ---
>
> **correlate**
> In scientific studies, when two things are observed together (which is not the same as one thing causing the other).

Psychopathy

A psychopath (or sociopath, as these terms are often used interchangeably) is a person who is incapable of feeling empathy. Most people associate psychopathy with serial killers like Ted Bundy or Jeffrey Dahmer—predators who killed multiple people over an extended period of time for psychological gratification. While most experts believe that all serial killers are psychopaths, very few psychopaths are serial killers. Psychologists believe about 1 percent of the US population (about 3 million people) are psychopaths, but the FBI estimates that there are only between twenty-five and fifty serial killers operating in the United States at any given time. However, this does not mean that psychopaths are harmless. As psychologist Marisa Brown explains, "The lack

Convicted serial killer Jeffrey Dahmer listens calmly at his murder trial. Psychopaths like Dahmer are able to commit their crimes because they are incapable of feeling empathy for others; this trait makes even those psychopaths who are not killers dangerous because they have no reluctance to hurt other people.

of empathy is what makes such individuals dangerous, since their reduced empathy makes it is easier for them to hurt others."[68]

Psychologist Robert Hare has been studying psychopaths for most of his career. He was the first to discover that the brains of psychopaths are markedly different from the brains of others. When psychopaths are shown disturbing photographs of human suffering, the emotional systems in their brains are not activated. In fact, fMRI imaging has revealed that viewing these images activates the ventral striatum, a brain structure associated with pleasure. According to neurobiologist Jean Decety, who conducted such a study in 2013, psychopaths seem to "find the distress of others pleasurable or positively arousing."[69]

Psychopaths do not just have a lack of empathy. Their entire emotional range tends to be blunted. Emotions like fear, anger, love, joy, and guilt do not motivate psychopaths—if they feel them at all. Instead, most psychopaths are motivated by the desire to acquire power over others. That power can take many forms. Some acquire wealth or seek out leadership positions, others pursue sexual conquests, and still others get pleasure from harming animals or people. While experts do not understand why this drive for power is so strong in psychopaths, some speculate that dominating others is the only way a psychopath can feel pleasure. For instance, serial killer David Krueger (also known as Peter Woodcock) describes killing as the ultimate rush: "I felt like God, [like I had] the power of God over a human being. . . . In the strangling of children I felt a degree and a sensation of pleasure, and of accomplishment, that I didn't feel anywhere else."[70]

Some psychologists have tried to treat violent psychopaths by asking them to do exercises designed to increase their empathy. Unfortunately, these therapies only helped psychopaths refine their manipulative abilities and made them more likely to reoffend. Krueger underwent this type of therapy in the 1970s and was thought to be so improved that he was transferred to a less-secure facility. Of that therapy, Krueger said, "I did learn how to manipulate better. I learned how to get control of expressing my feelings inappropriately . . . and keep the more outrageous feelings under wraps."[71] When Krueger was finally given a day pass—his first in thirty years—he brutally murdered a fellow inmate.

Today psychologists believe that psychopathy is caused by a genetic abnormality that can be identified by fMRI imaging and genetic testing. People with this abnormality are not necessarily violent. Experts believe that many of these nonviolent psychopaths have successfully integrated themselves into society. According to psychologist Kevin Dutton, psychopaths often excel as chief executive officers, lawyers, surgeons, and in other careers in which fearless decisiveness and a lack of empathy are an advantage.

Some psychologists believe that people born with psychopathy usually will not become violent predators unless they are exposed to extreme trauma, abuse, or neglect as children. For instance, neurosurgeon James Fallon has the genetic markers and brain patterns of a psychopath. Fallon, who had a happy and uneventful childhood, admits that he does not feel empathy and has many other psychopathic traits, but he claims he has no desire to be violent. As he speculates, "If I hadn't been treated so well, I probably wouldn't have made it out of being a teenager . . . because I would have been a violent guy."[72]

People with psychopathy, personality disorders, or mental illnesses do commit violent acts, but most violence is committed by people without these conditions. In fact, in most cases of violence, perpetrators are perfectly ordinary individuals who have either been overwhelmed by rage or caught up in the violent behavior of their in-group. Everyone has the capacity for violence, but most people will not commit acts of violence unless triggered or conditioned to do so.

SOURCE NOTES

Introduction: Is Violent Behavior Declining?

1. R. Douglas Fields, "Humans Are Genetically Predisposed to Kill Each Other," *The New Brain* (blog), *Psychology Today*, October 2, 2016. www.psychologytoday.com.
2. Jennifer Mascia, "15 Statistics That Tell the Story of Gun Violence This Year," Trace, March 15, 2017. www.thetrace.org.
3. Luke Glowacki, "Are People Violent By Nature? Probably," *Los Angeles Times*, January 19, 2014. http://articles.latimes.com.
4. Quoted in John Laidler, "Violence in Streets, Hope in the Data," *Harvard Gazette*, November 23, 2015. http://news.harvard.edu.
5. Quoted in Roy Speckhardt, "Giving Peace a Chance," *Huffington Post*, March 31, 2015. www.huffingtonpost.com.
6. Steven Pinker, "TED Talk—a Brief History of Violence," YouTube, December 31, 2015. www.youtube.com/watch?v=czNdHiQlQiU.
7. Quoted in Alex Gorlach, "The World Is Not as Bad as We Think, Says Harvard Psychologist," *Huffington Post*, August 8, 2016. www.huffingtonpost.com.
8. Steve Taylor, "The Psychology of War," *Out of the Darkness* (blog), *Psychology Today*, March 5, 2014. www.psychologytoday.com.

Chapter 1: The Brain, Evolution, and the Rage Response

9. R. Douglas Fields, *Why We Snap: Understanding the Rage Circuit in Your Brain*. New York: Dutton, 2015, p. 9.
10. Fields, *Why We Snap*, p. 6.
11. Fields, *Why We Snap*, p. 12.
12. Laura Hayes, "Can We Have Compassion for the Angry?," *Slate*, June 28, 2016. www.slate.com.
13. Hayes, "Can We Have Compassion for the Angry?"
14. Hayes, "Can We Have Compassion for the Angry?"
15. Melanie Greenberg, "Changing Your Brain by Changing Your Mind," Pathways Counseling Services, March 12, 2015. http://pathwayscounselingsvcs.com.

16. Glowacki, "Are People Violent by Nature?"

17. Quoted in James Hamblin, "The New American Face," *Atlantic*, November 21, 2016. www.theatlantic.com.

18. Quoted in Thomas DeMichele, "In-Groups and Out-Groups Explained," *Fact/Myth* (blog), March 20, 2016. http://fact myth.com.

19. Quoted in Hamblin, "The New American Face."

20. Justin Berg, "Is Racial Identity Based in Biology or Society?," Sociology in Focus, February 13, 2017. http://sociologyin focus.com.

21. Quoted in "Shooters Quicker to Pull Trigger When Target Is Black, Study Finds," National Public Radio, August 29, 2015. www.npr.org.

22. Cari Romm, "Rethinking One of Psychology's Most Infamous Experiments," *Atlantic*, January 28, 2015. www.theatlantic.com.

23. Quoted in Kathryn Millard, "Psychologists Say Milgram's Famous Experiment on Obedience to Authority Has Been Misunderstood," Medical Xpress, September 5, 2014. https://medicalxpress.com.

24. Quoted in Millard, "Psychologists Say Milgram's Famous Experiment on Obedience to Authority Has Been Misunderstood."

25. S. Alexander Haslam et al., "'Happy to Have Been of Service': The Yale Archives as a Window into the Engaged Followership of Participants in Milgram's 'Obedience' Experiments," *British Journal of Social Psychology*, September 5, 2014. http://onlinelibrary.wiley.com.

26. Quoted in Omer Bartov, "Defining Enemies, Making Victims: Germans, Jews, and the Holocaust," Academic Room, March 11, 2013. www.academicroom.com.

27. David Livingstone Smith, "Dehumanization: Psychological Aspects," Eugenics Archive, July 29, 2014. http://eugenics archive.ca.

28. Quoted in Robert Benz, "Race Delusion: Lies That Divide Us," *Huffington Post*, May 31, 2016. www.huffingtonpost.com.

29. Quoted in David Livingstone Smith, "Paradoxes of Dehumanization," *Social Theory and Practice*, April 2016, p. 433.

30. Quoted in Smith, "Paradoxes of Dehumanization," p. 426.
31. Smith, "Paradoxes of Dehumanization," p. 426.
32. Kendra Cherry, "What Is Operant Conditioning and How Does It Work?," Verywell, June 9, 2016. www.verywell.com.
33. Quoted in Jon, "Why Boot Camp Won't 'Brainwash' Recruits," War Elephant, September 12, 2015. https://war-elephant.com.
34. Quoted in Dave Grossman, *On Killing: The Psychological Cost of Learning to Kill in War and Society*. New York: Open Road Media, 2014. Kindle edition.
35. Grossman, *On Killing*.
36. Quoted in Oren Dorell, "Here's How the Islamic State Turns Children into Terrorists," *USA Today*, August 22, 2016. www.usatoday.com.
37. Michael Shermer, "Are We All Potentially Evil? A New Dramatic Film Based on the Stanford Prison Experiment Reveals Why Good People Turn Bad," *Huffington Post*, July 27, 2016. www.huffingtonpost.com.
38. Quoted in Matthew Sedacca, "The Man Who Played with Absolute Power," *Nautilus*, February 16, 2017. http://m.nautil.us.
39. Quoted in Jason Xidias, "Are Terrorists 'Evil'? Philip Zimbardo and the Darkness Within Us All," MACAT, June 7, 2016. www.macat.com.
40. Quoted in TommyGuns, "Abuse and Authority—the Abu Ghraib Comparison," Soapboxie, September 27, 2016. https://soapboxie.com.
41. Quoted in Theo Merz, "Sebastian Junger: 'War Gives Men a Sense of Purpose and Energy,'" *Telegraph* (London), June 3, 2014. www.telegraph.co.uk.
42. Taylor, "The Psychology of War."
43. Quoted in Jesse Singal, "Why ISIS Is So Terrifyingly Effective at Seducing New Recruits," *New York*, August 18, 2014. http://nymag.com.
44. Quoted in Singal, "Why ISIS Is So Terrifyingly Effective at Seducing New Recruits."

45. Christine Suhan, "13 Years After Being Raped, I Still Struggled with PTSD in My Marriage," *Good Housekeeping*, June 7, 2016. www.goodhousekeeping.com.

46. Suhan, "13 Years After Being Raped, I Still Struggled with PTSD in My Marriage."

47. *Merriam-Webster*, "Trauma," 2017. www.merriam-webster.com.

48. Viatcheslav Wlassoff, "How Does Post-Traumatic Stress Disorder Change the Brain?," *Brain Blogger*, January 24, 2015. http://brainblogger.com.

49. Wlassoff, "How Does Post-Traumatic Stress Disorder Change the Brain?"

50. Quoted in Quil Lawrence, "After Combat Stress, Violence Can Show Up at Home," NPR, April 27, 2016. www.npr.org.

51. Quoted in Lawrence, "After Combat Stress, Violence Can Show Up at Home."

52. Wlassoff, "How Does Post-Traumatic Stress Disorder Change the Brain?"

53. Wlassoff, "How Does Post-Traumatic Stress Disorder Change the Brain?"

54. Quoted in Maria Konnikova, "Trying to Cure Depression, but Inspiring Torture," *New Yorker*, January 14, 2015. www.newyorker.com.

55. Shane O'Mara, "Mind Games," *Foreign Affairs*, January 15, 2016. www.foreignaffairs.com.

56. O'Mara, "Mind Games."

57. Beverly Engel, "Healing the Shame of Childhood Abuse Through Self-Compassion," *The Compassion Chronicles* (blog), *Psychology Today*, January 15, 2015. www.psychologytoday.com.

58. Lauren Isaac, "Domestic Violence in Families: Theory, Effects, and Intervention," *Social Justice Solutions*, June 25, 2015. www.socialjusticesolutions.org.

59. Kendra Cherry, "Bobo Doll Experiment," Verywell, April 15, 2016. www.verywell.com.

60. Quoted in Tara Culp-Ressler, "The Hidden Consequences of Domestic Violence Lingers for Decades," *ThinkProgress* (blog), September 26, 2014. https://thinkprogress.org.

61. Hayes, "Can We Have Compassion for the Angry?"
62. Quoted in American Psychological Association, "Mental Illness Not Usually Linked to Crime, Research Finds," April 21, 2014. www.apa.org.
63. Quoted in Carolina A. Klein and Soniya Hirachan, "The Masks of Identities: Who's Who? Delusional Misidentification Syndromes," *Journal of the American Academy of Psychiatry and the Law*, September 2014. http://jaapl.org.
64. Phillip J. Resnick, "From Paranoid Fear to Completed Homicide," *Current Psychiatry*, February 15, 2016. www.mdedge.com.
65. Betsy Seifter, "Schizophrenia and Violence, Part II," *After the Diagnosis* (blog), *Psychology Today*, February 27, 2015. www.psychologytoday.com.
66. Neel Burton, "The 10 Personality Disorders," *Hide and Seek* (blog), *Psychology Today*, August 21, 2015. www.psychologytoday.com.
67. Quoted in Rick Nauert, "Low Empathy Associated with Borderline Personality Disorder," Psych Central, August 31, 2015. https://psychcentral.com.
68. Marisa Brown, "Toward a Neurobiological Understanding of Antisocial and Psychopathic Personalities and the Particular Role of Empathy," Exploring Mental Health, April 22, 2014. https://campuspress.yale.edu.
69. Quoted in Brown, "Toward a Neurobiological Understanding of Antisocial and Psychopathic Personalities and the Particular Role of Empathy."
70. Quoted in BBC, *The Mystery of Murder: A Horizon Guide*, documentary, 2015. www.dailymotion.com.
71. Quoted in BBC, *The Mystery of Murder*.
72. Quoted in Judith Ohikuare, "Life as a Nonviolent Psychopath," *Atlantic*, January 21, 2014. www.theatlantic.com.

FOR FURTHER RESEARCH

Books

Alex Alvarez and Ronet Bachman, *Violence: The Enduring Problem*, 3rd ed. Thousand Oaks, CA: Sage, 2017.

Richard Bessel, *Violence: A Modern Obsession*. New York: Simon & Schuster, 2016.

Paul Bloom, *Against Empathy: The Case for Rational Compassion*. New York: HarperCollins, 2016.

R. Douglas Fields, *Why We Snap: Understanding the Rage Circuit in Your Brain*. New York: Dutton, 2015.

Dave Grossman, *On Killing: The Psychological Cost of Learning to Kill in War and Society*. New York: Open Road Media, 2014. Kindle edition.

Internet Sources

Marisa Brown, "Toward a Neurobiological Understanding of Antisocial and Psychopathic Personalities and the Particular Role of Empathy," Exploring Mental Health, April 22, 2014. https:// campuspress.yale.edu/exploringmentalhealth/toward-a-neuro biological-understanding-of-antisocial-and-psychopathic-per sonalities-and-the-particular-role-of-empathy.

Luke Glowacki, "Are People Violent By Nature? Probably," *Los Angeles Times*, January 19, 2014. http://articles.latimes.com/2014 /jan/19/opinion/la-oe-glowacki-violence-humans-genes-2014 0119.

Laura Hayes, "Can We Have Compassion for the Angry?," *Slate*, June 28, 2016. www.slate.com/articles/health_and_science/med ical_examiner/2016/06/the_biggest_predictor_of_future_violence _is_past_violence_but_mindfulness.html.

Judith Ohikuare, "Life as a Nonviolent Psychopath," *Atlantic*, January 21, 2014. www.theatlantic.com/health/archive/2014/01/life -as-a-nonviolent-psychopath/282271.

Shane O'Mara, "Mind Games," *Foreign Affairs*, January 15, 2016. www.foreignaffairs.com/articles/2016-01-15/mind-games.

Cari Romm, "Rethinking One of Psychology's Most Infamous Experiments," *Atlantic*, January 28, 2015. www.theatlantic.com /health/archive/2015/01/rethinking-one-of-psychologys-most -infamous-experiments/384913.

Jason Xidias, "Are Terrorists 'Evil'? Philip Zimbardo and the Darkness Within Us All," MACAT, June 7, 2016. www.macat.com /blog/are-terrorists-evil-zimbardo.

Websites

Big Think (https://bigthink.com). Big Think presents the ideas of the world's most renowned scientists, philosophers, and other experts. The website includes hundreds of videos and articles that explore violence from psychological, neurological, and sociological perspectives.

Brain Blogger (https://brainblogger.com). Brain Blogger is produced by the Global Neuroscience Initiative Foundation. The website includes hundreds of articles that explore violence from the perspectives of psychology, neuroscience, and health.

Psychology Today (http://www.psychologytoday.com). *Psychology Today* explores psychological issues through articles, blogs, and expert interviews. Its website includes hundreds of articles related to violence.